An Autumn Treasury

of Recipes, Crafts and Wisdom

ANGELA
FERRARO-FANNING

ANNELIESDRAWS

IVY KIDS

CONTENTS

WELCOME TO AUTUMN AT THE LITTLE COUNTRY COTTAGE!

Autumn is a very exciting season because it is harvest time! After all of our planning, planting, growing and tending, we can finally pick so many of the fruits and vegetables that we have been growing since spring.

This season, the animals scurry about, readying for winter, and so do we! Our baskets are filled with pumpkins and gourds. Wild mushrooms are foraged and fresh apples and pears are plucked from the trees. Seeds are saved for spring, and herbs are gathered and dried.

It's a perfect time for craft projects and home baking and there are many fun ways to make the most of nature's gifts during this season.

Turn the pages and see how you can join in!

WE LOVE AUTUMN!

The days are warm and filled with golden sunlight, and the leaves on the trees are bursting with colour. The nights are becoming chilly, and birds and wildlife are busy gathering nuts and seeds to store before the cold ahead. There is much to see, enjoy and explore!

As **DAYLIGHT SHORTENS**, the leaves change colour

Home-grown **APPLES** are ripe for picking

PUMPKINS can be picked and roasted

FALLEN LEAVES are waiting to be jumped in

SUNFLOWER SEEDS are ready to harvest

SQUIRRELS are busy gathering nuts for winter

POPCORN COBS are ready for picking and drying

The animals enjoy the **COOLER WEATHER**

5

AUTUMN CROPS: APPLES AND PEARS

Have you ever tasted an apple or pear picked fresh from the tree?
The trees blossom in the spring and, if bees find the flowers, they produce
fruit that begins as small as a marble. All spring and summer long they
slowly grow. Come the autumn, these colourful, nutritious fruits are
finally ready for picking and savouring.

Apple and pear trees have a special relationship with
honeybees. The tree needs the bees' help in pollinating their
flowers. The transfer of pollen by the honeybee from one
blossom to another is how fruit begins to grow.

But the bees also need the pollen and nectar
from the tree. They take this tasty pollen and
nectar back to their hive and save it as food in
their comb. The nectar is shared by the bees and
made into honey.

Honey created from apple or pear blossoms is very
light in colour and has a sweet and floral flavour.

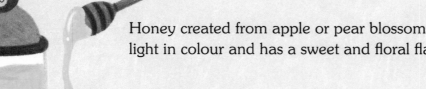

RECIPE FOR CINNAMON APPLE SAUCE

Homemade apple sauce is an easy to make, healthy treat that's full of goodness. It's also a great way to use up any bruised or misshapen apples so nothing goes to waste. Be sure to ask a grown-up for help when it comes to chopping, peeling and cooking on the hob. This recipe makes enough sauce to fill about five jam jars.

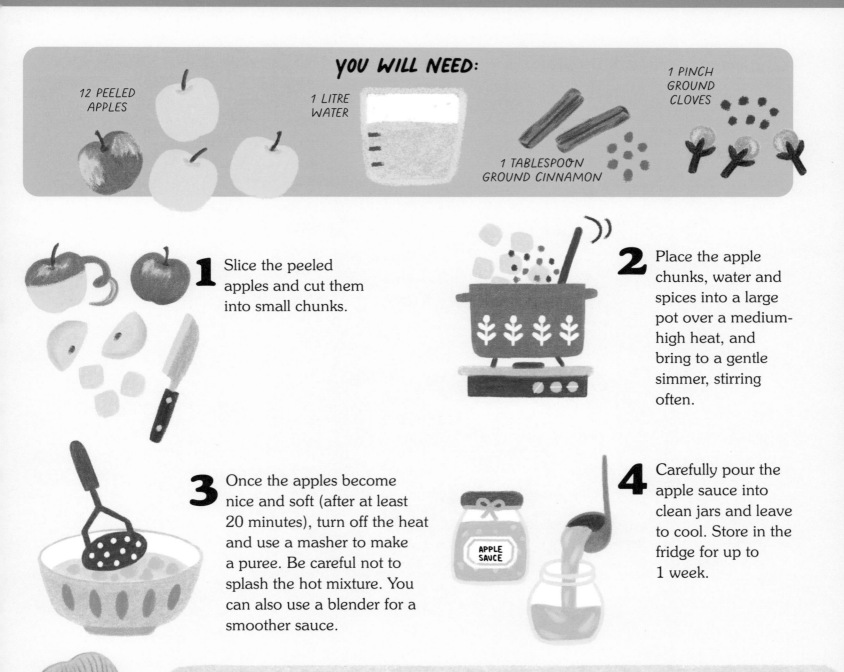

YOU WILL NEED:

12 PEELED APPLES

1 LITRE WATER

1 TABLESPOON GROUND CINNAMON

1 PINCH GROUND CLOVES

1 Slice the peeled apples and cut them into small chunks.

2 Place the apple chunks, water and spices into a large pot over a medium-high heat, and bring to a gentle simmer, stirring often.

3 Once the apples become nice and soft (after at least 20 minutes), turn off the heat and use a masher to make a puree. Be careful not to splash the hot mixture. You can also use a blender for a smoother sauce.

4 Carefully pour the apple sauce into clean jars and leave to cool. Store in the fridge for up to 1 week.

APPLE SAUCE

TIP: FOR AN EXTRA VITAMIN BOOST, LEAVE THE SKINS ON THE APPLES. SOFT APPLE VARIETIES LIKE GOLDEN DELICIOUS, MCINTOSH AND FUJI ARE BEST FOR THIS RECIPE, BECAUSE THEY BREAK DOWN EASILY.

APPLE AND PEAR VARIETIES

Do you have a favourite kind of apple or pear? These autumnal fruits grow in all different colours and shapes. They can be sweet, tart, soft, crisp. Some are perfect for baking and cooking, while others are just right for eating fresh.

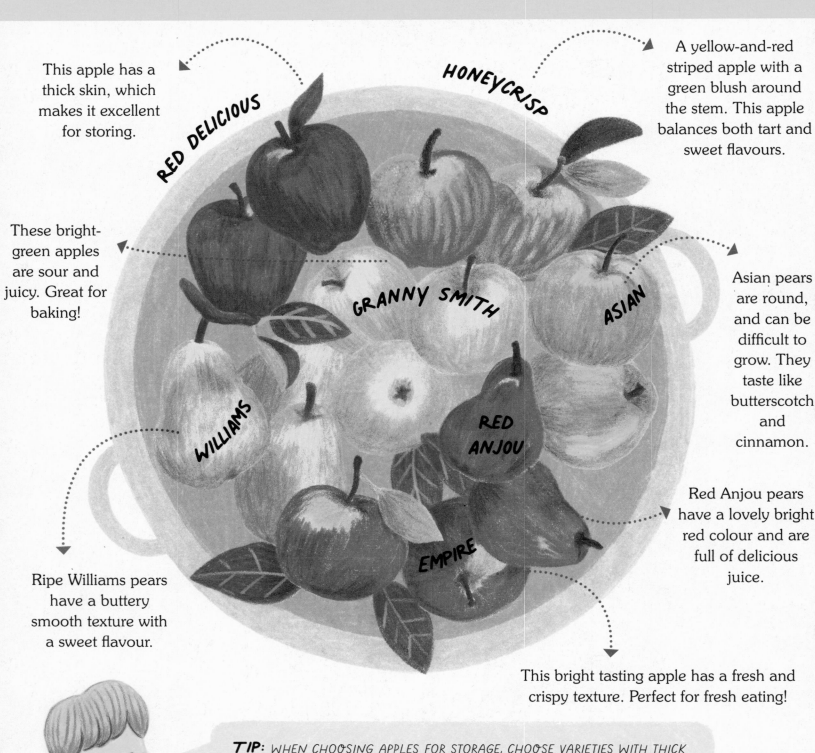

This apple has a thick skin, which makes it excellent for storing.

RED DELICIOUS

HONEYCRISP

A yellow-and-red striped apple with a green blush around the stem. This apple balances both tart and sweet flavours.

These bright-green apples are sour and juicy. Great for baking!

GRANNY SMITH

ASIAN

Asian pears are round, and can be difficult to grow. They taste like butterscotch and cinnamon.

WILLIAMS

RED ANJOU

Red Anjou pears have a lovely bright red colour and are full of delicious juice.

EMPIRE

Ripe Williams pears have a buttery smooth texture with a sweet flavour.

This bright tasting apple has a fresh and crispy texture. Perfect for fresh eating!

TIP: WHEN CHOOSING APPLES FOR STORAGE, CHOOSE VARIETIES WITH THICK SKIN. TART APPLES STORE LONGER THAN SWEET APPLES, TOO.

RECIPE FOR APPLE CHIPS

When stored at a cool temperature, apples can stay fresh for months, but these crispy, dried apple chips are a super-fun way to make apples last – as long as you don't eat them all at once! For safety, make sure to ask a grown-up for help.

YOU WILL NEED:

APPLES — AS MANY AS YOU LIKE!

1 Wash and dry the apples, then cut each one into four large sections. Remove the cores and stems. Thinly slice the sections, about 1 centimetre wide. The thinner the slices are, the crispier the chips will be!

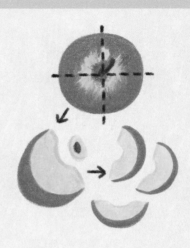

2 If you have a dehydrator, lay the slices on the racks. If not, place them on baking trays lined with greaseproof paper. Make sure the slices don't overlap.

3 Dehydrate the apples for 10 hours at 65°C. If baking in the oven, cook at 90°C for 1 hour, then flip the slices and bake for another 1 ½ hours, or until the chips are crispy, but not brown.

4 When the slices are fully dried and crisp, remove them. They're now ready to taste and crunch! You can store leftovers in an airtight container for up to 1 week.

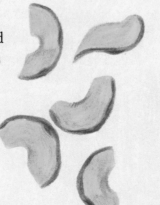

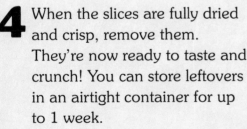

TIP: FOR ADDED FLAVOUR, TRY SPRINKLING THE APPLES WITH GROUND CINNAMON OR VANILLA BEAN SUGAR BEFORE YOU DRY THEM.

USES FOR CORES, SEEDS AND PEELS

You might be used to throwing apple and pear cores and peels away, but did you know there are many handy ways to use them? Take a look at four examples...

GROW YOUR OWN APPLE TREE

It's possible to grow your very own apple tree using the seeds of an apple.

YOU WILL NEED:
- A SMALL PLANT POT
- POTTING SOIL
- 1 APPLE SEED
- WATER

1 Remove an apple seed from an apple core and rinse with water.

2 Fill your pot with potting soil and insert the seed about 2 centimetres into the soil.

3 Cover lightly with more soil, then water it.

4 Choose a sunny, sheltered spot for your tree, and water daily to keep the soil moist.

5 Watch your apple tree grow! As it gets bigger, you can plant it in your garden, or repot it using a bigger pot.

FEED ANIMALS

Cores and peels can be fed to farm animals like pigs, horses and chickens. Pets such as hamsters, rabbits and guinea pigs enjoy crunchy peels, too.

BREW TASTY TEA

Place a slice of apple or pear peel in a teacup, or several slices in a teapot, then fill with hot water for a delicious tea that will warm you up during the chilly autumn evenings.

MAKE POTPOURRI

Dry the cores and peels using a dehydrator, or by baking in the oven on a low heat for a few hours. Add a cinnamon stick to the dried peels and cores, then place in a bowl to give your home a wonderful autumnal scent!

AUTUMN CROPS: PUMPKINS AND GOURDS

Autumn is a time of colour and fun. Finally, the pumpkins and gourds that have grown all summer long are ready for picking! These crops grow in all kinds of shapes and sizes, and their skin (called a rind) can come in many different colours.

PUMPKINS

Pumpkins are popular all over the world. Many are edible – meaning you can eat them. Lots of people also use them to carve faces and pictures at Halloween.

CINDERELLA
Large reddish pumpkins named after Cinderella's carriage! They have a creamy, slightly sweet flavour.

BLUE DOLL
Super sweet and great for baking and roasting. This pumpkin's rind is a green/blue colour, while the flesh inside is orange.

SUGAR PIE
Small and tasty pumpkins. Perfect for pies and soups.

JACK O'LANTERN
These pumpkins are great for carving.

WARTY GOBLIN
These spooky pumpkins are covered in wartlike bumps – perfect to display on Halloween.

BABY BOO
These white, palm-sized pumpkins, aren't edible, but they can be used as decorations for autumn-themed displays.

GOURDS

Gourds, like pumpkins, have a hard skin. Unlike pumpkins, most gourds are not grown for eating but for craft projects. Gourds can be turned into birdhouses, bottles, spoons – even musical instruments!

SPECKLED SWAN
The long, curved neck of this gourd looks like a swan's neck!

SHENOT CROWN OF THORNS
These beautiful crown-shaped gourds can be orange, white, yellow, green, striped and multi-coloured.

BIRDHOUSE
These funny-shaped gourds are perfect for turning into bottles and birdhouses.

RECIPE FOR SWEET PUMPKIN MUFFINS

Pumpkin muffins are a delicious autumnal treat. Follow the steps below to bake a scrumptious batch of 12. Be sure to ask a grown-up for help.

YOU WILL NEED:

- 1 LARGE SUGAR PIE PUMPKIN OR 225 GRAMS TINNED PUMPKIN PUREE (UNSWEETENED)
- BLENDER (IF MAKING PUREE)
- MUFFIN TINS

- 225 GRAMS PLAIN FLOUR (SIFTED)
- 1 TEASPOON BAKING POWDER
- 5 TABLESPOONS VEGETABLE OIL
- 110 GRAMS UNSWEETENED APPLE SAUCE
- ½ TEASPOON GROUND CINNAMON

- ¼ TEASPOON GROUND CLOVES
- ¼ TEASPOON GROUND ALLSPICE
- ½ TEASPOON BICARBONATE OF SODA
- 225 GRAMS WHITE GRANULATED SUGAR

1 If you're using tinned puree, skip to Step 2. If you're making the puree, wash and dry your pumpkin, then ask a grown-up to cut it in half. Put the halves, cut side down, on a baking tray lined with greaseproof paper and roast for 45 minutes, or until the flesh is soft. Scoop out the roasted flesh and blend until smooth.

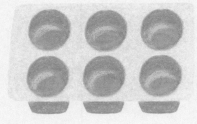

2 Preheat the oven to 180°C. Grease your muffin tins – you can use a little coconut oil, vegetable oil or butter for this.

3 Combine all the ingredients in a bowl. Whisk together for about 2 to 3 minutes, until smooth. Don't over mix.

4 Spoon the mixture into each cup in the muffin tins. Each cup should be about half-full.

5 Bake for 15 to 20 minutes. To see if the muffins are ready, insert a toothpick into the centre of a muffin – if it comes out clean, the muffins are baked. If not, bake for a little longer, then try again.

6 Once baked, sprinkle a little extra sugar on the tops, or leave plain, then cool for 5 minutes before turning them out onto a cooling rack. Once they're cool, take a big bite!

USES FOR PUMPKIN SEEDS

Inside a pumpkin, you can find its seeds. Don't throw them away! The seeds are super useful, and there are many ways to make the most of them.

ROASTED PUMPKIN SEEDS

This crunchy snack is easy to make and easy to eat! Place the seeds evenly on a baking tray lined with greaseproof paper. Drizzle with olive oil and your favourite seasonings. Toss so all the seeds are coated evenly, then roast in the oven at 180°C for 15 to 20 minutes, until just turning brown and a little crispy.

CHILLI FLAKES

SALT

PEPPER

FENNEL SEEDS

GARLIC POWDER

ONION POWDER

PAPRIKA

MAKE A MARACA

Did you know pumpkin seeds can be musical? When fully dried, sprinkle a few pumpkin seeds inside a small container with a lid. Shake the seeds and hear the music!

SAVE AND GROW

In the spring, fill a small flowerpot that has a hole for drainage with seed-starting soil. Plant the seed about 2 centimetres deep and cover loosely with soil. Place in a sunny location. Keep the soil moist by watering regularly. Soon, a new pumpkin vine will grow!

MAKE PESTO SAUCE

Ask a grown-up to help combine 120 millilitres olive oil, 60 grams fresh basil leaves, 2 whole garlic cloves, 2 tablespoons lemon juice, ½ teaspoon salt, ¼ teaspoon black pepper and 50 grams of pumpkin seeds in a blender or food processor. Blend until smooth and enjoy on top of fresh-cooked pasta or warm bread!

MAKE A BIRDHOUSE FROM A GOURD

Have you heard of a birdhouse gourd? Once dry, these crops are perfect for creating homes for birds and small animals. This craft project is so fun and easy, plus it gives our little friends in nature a safe space to enjoy. Remember to ask a grown-up for help when using the tools.

YOU WILL NEED:

- 1 BIRDHOUSE GOURD, FULLY DRIED AND HARDENED (AVAILABLE AT FARM AND GARDENING SHOPS)
- 1 PENCIL
- 1 SMALL HAMMER
- 1 LONG NAIL
- 1 HOOK (IF HANGING)
- STRING (IF HANGING)

1 Draw a 5-centimetre wide circle onto the gourd with a pencil, where you would like the doorway to be. Using a hammer, gently pound a nail into the gourd somewhere along the pencil line. (Just a few taps of the hammer to puncture the rind.) Remove the nail and repeat all the way around the circle.

2 Now that the circle is punctured with nail holes, it's time to punch out the door! Using your hammer, give a gentle tap in the centre of the circle. Keep tapping until the circle falls inwards.

3 Turn the gourd over and shake out all the dried bits and seeds through the hole. Ask a grown-up to secure a hook into the top of the gourd. Now it's ready to hang from a tree or balcony! Alternatively, you could leave it on the ground outside, for teeny land animals to enjoy.

TIP: YOU CAN DECORATE THE OUTSIDE OF YOUR GOURD WITH NON-TOXIC PAINT.

DEER AND WILDLIFE

If you have a big garden or a forest nearby, you can leave your pumpkins in nature. Deer and other wild animals will be so happy to find these tasty treats in the forest.

PIGS, SHEEP AND HORSES

With a grown-up, you can offer spare pumpkins to local farms. Farmers can feed these yummy crops to all kinds of animals.

TIP: PUMPKINS SHOULD ALWAYS BE FRESH AND FREE OF MOULD, NOT ROTTEN. THEY SHOULD ALSO HAVE NO PAINT, CHEMICALS OR ACCESSORIES THAT MIGHT HURT THE ANIMALS.

PUMPKINS FOR THE ANIMALS

Did you know that many animals love the taste of pumpkin just as much as people do? Orange pumpkins (never white ones) are a very healthy treat. They contain lots of vitamins and a special property called cucurbitacin, which fights off worms that can make animals sick. Here are some ways to share your pumpkins!

CHICKENS AND DUCKS

Ducks and chickens love pumpkin. You can split a pumpkin in half and simply give it to the flock. It's so fun to watch them peck and eat the pulp and seeds!

DOGS AND CATS

Raw and cooked pumpkin flesh and seeds are safe for dogs, while cooked pumpkin flesh and seeds are best for cats. The ingredients can be stirred in with their food or pureed in a blender and then fed to our furry friends.

Some wild mushrooms are poisonous or unsafe to eat. Never pick or eat a wild mushroom.

The part of the mushroom that we see and pick is the fruit. Underground is the 'mycelium' – a very large root system.

Unlike most plants, mushrooms don't need sunlight to grow. They thrive in the shade or other dark spaces.

AUTUMN CROP: MUSHROOMS

Many mushroom varieties spring up from the earth, ready for harvesting in the autumn. The wet rains and the warm daytime temperatures of this season are a perfect recipe for mushroom growing! Mushrooms are made of mostly water and come in all different shapes, sizes and colours.

Some mushrooms and trees work together. The mushroom helps the tree take in water and nutrients. In return, the tree releases sugars that feed the mushroom.

Mushrooms are great at making the air cleaner. They also help to break down dead matter and return energy into the soil.

Some mushrooms can glow in the dark!

MAKE A MUSHROOM LOG

In the wild, many mushrooms like to grow on trees and logs. We can do the same thing in our homes or gardens! Follow the simple steps to make your own mushroom logs. For safety, make sure to ask a grown-up for help.

YOU WILL NEED:

- 1 HARDWOOD LOG (OAK, MAPLE, BEECH, ETC.), AT LEAST 12 CENTIMETRES IN DIAMETER AND 1 METRE LONG
- EDIBLE MUSHROOM SPAWN DOWELS (AVAILABLE ONLINE AND FROM GARDENING SHOPS)
- HAMMER
- 2-CENTIMETRE DRILL BIT
- HAND OR POWER DRILL
- WAX FOR MELTING (BEESWAX, SOY, ETC.)

1 Ask a grown-up to help you drill holes roughly 2 centimetres deep into your log. Holes should be spaced roughly 10 centimetres apart so as not to overcrowd your mushrooms.

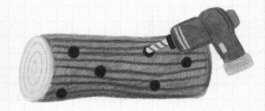

3 Melt the wax on the hob then brush the melted wax over each of the filled holes. Place your log indoors, away from a window, or outdoors in a shady spot.

5 Be patient! It usually takes about one year for the mushrooms to sprout. Once they do, you can pick, cook and enjoy them. After the first sprouting, the log should produce mushrooms once or twice a year, for up to seven years!

2 After the holes have been drilled, it's time to insert the spawn! Grab a dowel and place it in the hole. Gently hammer it all the way in. Repeat until all of the holes have been filled.

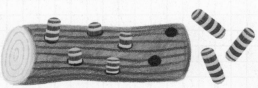

4 Using a watering can or hose, sprinkle the log. This waters the mushroom spawn. Water for 10 minutes, once or twice a week.

FACT: MUSHROOM DOWELS ARE LITTLE PIECES OF WOOD SOAKED WITH WATER AND MUSHROOM SPAWN. SPAWN ARE SIMILAR TO SEEDS.

ROSEMARY
A thick woody herb with pine-needle-like leaves.

CORIANDER
Looks very similar to parsley. A clean, slightly spicy flavour.

OREGANO
A savoury flavour often used in pizza sauce.

BASIL
Large green leaves and a licorice scent.

THYME
A woody stem with small, spicy scented leaves.

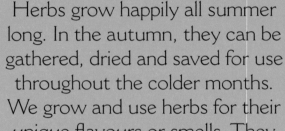

HERBS

Herbs grow happily all summer long. In the autumn, they can be gathered, dried and saved for use throughout the colder months. We grow and use herbs for their unique flavours or smells. They add spice and fragrance to meals, and can be used in perfume, soap and even medicine. Some have healing qualities and others attract bees and butterflies. Do you have a favourite herb?

DILL
Dill leaves and seeds are often used in pickle making.

PARSLEY
Leaves can be flat or curly.

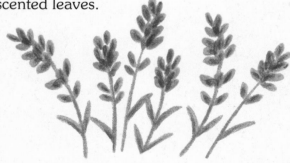

LAVENDER
Fragrant purple flowers and a favourite of bees and butterflies! Often used in soap.

CALENDULA
A beautiful flower that is edible and used for medicine. Can be eaten fresh in salads or dried and used in beauty products and tea.

GROW A WINDOWSILL HERB GARDEN

Did you know that we can grow herbs indoors just like flowers or other potted plants? Find a sunny windowsill and follow the simple steps to make your own herb garden.

YOU WILL NEED:

- HERB SEEDLINGS (A FEW DIFFERENT HERBS)
- 1 POT PER PLANT, WITH A HOLE AND TRAY
- POTTING MIX SOIL
- PLANT LABELS
- WASHABLE MARKER PENS

1 Pot one seedling at a time. Fill a pot with potting soil about half-way full. Then set the seedling in the pot, on top of the soil.

2 Add more potting soil into the pot, around the seedling. Ensure the roots are covered on all sides and on the top, then gently pat the soil into place.

FACT: SEEDLINGS ARE NEWLY-SPROUTED HERB SEEDS. YOU CAN FIND THEM AT MOST GARDENING SHOPS.

3 Place the pot on a sunny window ledge and place the drainage tray underneath. Water your newly potted herb to moisten the soil.

4 Decorate your herb label with the marker pens by writing the herb name and creating a fun design! Insert the label into the pot carefully.

BASIL

5 Repeat all the steps for the remaining seedlings. Watch your garden grow!

BUILD A HERB-DRYING BRANCH

Herbs taste and smell just as delicious when dried as when we harvest them from a fresh plant. One way we can dry herbs is to hang them upside down from a string. This allows the plant to keep its shape while getting lots of air flow. A neat way to dry herbs is by hanging bundles from a branch.

YOU WILL NEED:

- 1 LARGE BRANCH, FREE OF MOULD AND DIRT
- ROPE OR STRING FOR HANGING THE BRANCH
- FRESH HERBS OF YOUR CHOICE (GATHERED AND TIED INTO BUNCHES)
- CLOTHES PEGS
- HOOKS FOR THE WALL OR CEILING (OPTIONAL)

1 Decide with a grown-up on a space to hang your branch. Then find a branch that will fit that space and bring it indoors. Tie string around each end. This is how the branch will hang from the wall or ceiling.

2 Tie loops of string around the middle of the branch. The number of loops should match the number of herb bunches you want to hang. Make the loops different sizes.

3 With a grown-up's help, hang the branch. (If you're hanging the branch very high up, complete Step 4 first.)

4 It's time to hang the herbs! Use the clothes pegs to secure the bunches to the string loops. The different sizes of the loops will make the bunches hang at different heights, so they all have plenty of space to dry.

5 Allow the herbs to fully dry. Depending on the herb, this may take several weeks. Remove from the branch and crush the herbs. Store in an airtight container.

SAVING SEEDS

Seeds are magical! One little seed grows into a full-sized plant, providing us with flowers, food and nutrients. Imagine how rewarding it is when we grow plants from our very own seeds we've saved! Shelling beans, corn and sunflowers are all ready to harvest in the autumn. Here's how to save their seeds to grow again...

SHELLING BEANS

Instead of eating these beans fresh, we leave shelling beans on the vine to dry all summer long. We can use these dried beans later, in winter soups and stews, or we can save them. To do this, let the beans fully dry until the pods turn wrinkly, yellow or brown and crisp. Pull the pods from the vines. Open the pods and remove the beans. Spread them on some greaseproof paper and leave to dry in a cool, dark place for three weeks. They can then be stored in an airtight jar for cooking or placed in seed packets for growing next spring.

CORN

These seeds are the very same kernels that we eat from the cob. In order to save them, we need the cob to fully dry first. Place or hang the cob in a dry location. If we press into a kernel with our fingernail and there is no juice, we know that the corn is dried. Remove the dried kernels from the cob using your thumb. Let them dry for two more weeks in a single layer on a towel or piece of greaseproof paper. Keep them in a dry, dark place. They are then ready for packaging, or turning into tasty popcorn!

SUNFLOWER

When sunflowers begin to droop and their heads turn a pale green, yellow or brown, the blossoms are ready for harvesting. Simply cut off the flower heads from the large stalks and bring indoors to dry for a week. They may curl or warp slightly. Using your thumb, push away the pollen heads in the centre of the flower. The seeds will be hiding underneath! Loosen and remove these by rubbing the seeds with your fingers. Lay them out in a single layer to dry on greaseproof paper for two weeks before storing.

CREATE YOUR OWN SEED PACKETS

When our seeds are fully dried and ready to store until planting time in the spring, it's best to keep them in a paper envelope. Paper allows the seeds to breathe and lets any accidental moisture escape. This keeps mould away. Follow the steps to learn how to fold your own seed envelopes and decorate them, too!

YOU WILL NEED:

- THICK CRAFT PAPER IN DIFFERENT COLOURS OR PATTERNS, CUT INTO 15 X 20-CENTIMETRE RECTANGLES
- COLOURED MARKER PENS
- STICKY TAPE

1 Fold the paper in half, then unfold it. There should now be a crease down the middle.

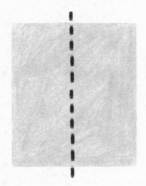

2 Fold the top two corners of the rectangles inwards towards the centre crease, to make a triangle at the top.

3 Fold the edges of both sides inwards, by about 2 centimetres.

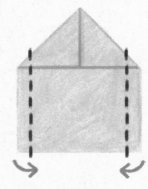

4 Fold the bottom of the paper up to meet the bottom of the triangle.

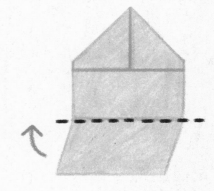

5 Tape the sides closed.

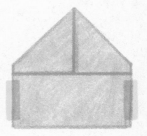

6 Place your seeds inside the envelope pocket. When ready, fold the top of the triangle down. You can use tape to secure the flap in place.

7 Decorate your seed packets with marker pens! Write the name of the plant, the date you saved them and where they came from.

FLOWER

CRAFT ACORN CAP CANDLES

Acorns are the sweet, nut-shaped seeds with little hats that drop from oak trees in the autumn. Squirrels and other wildlife love to gather and store them as food for the winter. The animals don't eat the 'hats', called caps, but we can use them to make tiny candle holders! For safety, make sure to ask a grown-up for help.

YOU WILL NEED:

- ACORN CAPS (CLEANED AND DRIED)
- A DINNER PLATE
- DRIED RICE
- WAX FOR MELTING (BEESWAX, SOY, ETC.)
- CANDLE WICKS (AVAILABLE AT CRAFT SHOPS)
- SCISSORS

1 Pour the dried rice on the plate. Place the acorn caps, bowl side up, into the rice – this will keep the caps stable.

3 Carefully dip the end of a wick into the melted wax, then quickly press the wax end of the wick into the centre of an acorn cap.

5 Once the wax has cooled for at least 10 minutes, use scissors to trim the wick to about 2 centimetres above the acorn cap.

2 Ask a grown-up to help melt wax on the hob, according to the package directions.

4 Using a spoon, carefully fill the cap with more melted wax. Hold the wick up in place for a moment, until the wax has set.

6 The candles are ready! As the bottoms are pointy, they won't lie flat on a surface. Instead, use them as floating candles in a bowl of water. Ask a grown-up to light them.

MAKE SOOTHING LIP BALM

The warm days of autumn are followed by chilly nights. This can take a toll on our lips and make them dry. Making our own lip balm is easy and we can make it extra special by choosing the flavours! Homemade lip balm also makes an excellent gift for friends and family. Follow the steps to see how to make your own.

YOU WILL NEED:

- 2 TABLESPOONS COCONUT OIL
- 1 TABLESPOON BEESWAX (GRATED OR BEADS)
- 10 DROPS PURE ESSENTIAL OILS (YOU CAN CHOOSE FROM MANY OPTIONS, INCLUDING LAVENDER, PEPPERMINT AND VANILLA)
- LIP BALM TUBES OR POTS (AVAILABLE AT CRAFT SHOPS)

1 In a microwave-safe bowl, combine the coconut oil and beeswax.

2 Place the bowl in the microwave and heat for 30 seconds. Stir. Repeat in 30-second increments until the wax is melted and the liquid is clear. Then, ask a grown-up to remove the hot liquid from the microwave.

3 Add the essential oil to the bowl and stir.

4 Ask a grown-up to pour the hot mixture into the containers. This recipe should fill about 10 small pots or tubes.

5 Allow the containers to cool and set completely, unsealed, for a few hours. When cool, the balm is ready for use!

WEAVE A MINI BASKET

In the autumn, our baskets are full of fresh, homegrown produce. Often the farmer has so many things to pick and collect, that they can run out of baskets quickly! Did you know that it's fun and easy to make baskets using a paper plate and some yarn? Follow the steps to weave your own mini basket.

YOU WILL NEED:

A PAPER PLATE

A PENCIL

SCISSORS

SOMETHING ROUND TO TRACE, SUCH AS A BOWL

YARN

1 Using a bowl, trace a circle in the centre of the paper plate. Then draw 9 lines from the circle to the outside edge. It's like drawing a sun with rays!

3 Widen each cut you've made by snipping a bit off of each side, creating a 'V' shape.

4 Fold each tab into the centre of the plate along the traced pencil line. When you let go, they will stand up, making a bowl shape. If any of the tabs overlap, be sure to cut off more to widen the gaps.

2 Using scissors, cut along each line until you reach your centre circle. Stop at the circle.

5 It's time to weave! Take a strand of yarn and hold the tail in the centre of the paper plate. Using your other hand, begin weaving the yarn through the tabs. Start by stringing the yarn behind one tab, then in front of the next. Repeat this 'over and under' weaving over and over around the circle. Avoid pulling too tight because it will warp the shape of the basket.

6 To change colour, simply tie a new strand of yarn to the yarn you are currently weaving with.

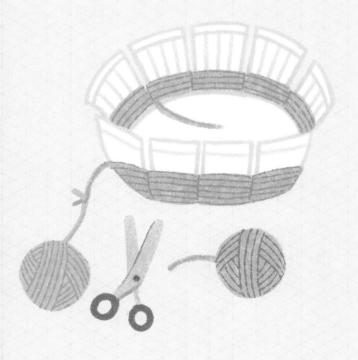

7 Once you've reached the top of the paper plate tabs, leave about 2 centimetres of the paper plate showing. Bend the tops of the tabs back, towards the outside of the basket just slightly. This will prevent the weaving from sliding off of the tabs!

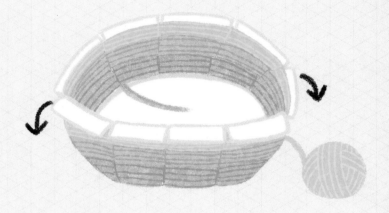

8 Tie off the end of your yarn, then use a pencil to tuck it, and any other ties that stick out, behind your weaving.

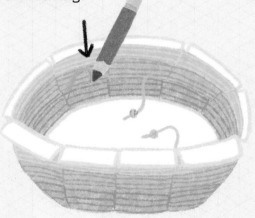

9 Fill your basket!

MAKE A GRATITUDE TREE

Autumn is a season for gratitude; a time to give thanks for all that Mother Nature has provided us with over the warmer months. One way to show thanks is to create a gratitude tree. A gratitude tree is simply a collection of thankful thoughts written on paper leaves and fixed to a branch. As we add leaves, our branch begins to fill and resemble a tree.

YOU WILL NEED:

- 1 BRANCH, WITH LOTS OF SMALLER SIDE BRANCHES
- 1 FLOWERPOT, ANY SIZE
- ROCKS (ENOUGH TO FILL THE POT AND STABILISE THE BRANCH)
- THICK CARD PAPER IN RED, YELLOW, ORANGE AND GREEN
- SCISSORS
- CLOTHES PEGS
- COLOURED MARKER PENS

1 Find a large fallen branch that has smaller side branches. Make sure it is clean of mould and debris before bringing it indoors.

2 Insert the branch into the centre of the flowerpot. Ask a friend to add rocks to the pot around the base of the branch while you hold it. Fill the pot all the way to the top. This will keep your branch upright and in place. When you let go, the branch should not fall.

3 Cut the paper into leaf shapes. Be sure each shape is large enough, with room for writing.